<u>INDEX</u>

Chapter One

Chapter Two

Iran's Intelligence

The priorities of the Iranian intelligence and security system seem to be directed towards the maintenance of domestic stability, the surveillance of foreign powers that could threaten Iran, the warning over possible actions and redirecting attention from them as well as the procurement of better defense capabilities.

The "secrecy" that characterizes the Iranian regime and organizations is specific to the intelligence services too. The president has more authority with the MOIS, one of the ministries of the government, while the IRGC has become a national institution under the leadership of Iran's Supreme Leader. Iran's Supreme National Security Council (SNSC) - the state official organization that makes foreign and military decisions and Supreme Leader's Intelligence Unit are two semi-collateral organizations that gather all the intelligence authorities. Their decisions must ultimately be approved by the Supreme Leader.

During the last two decades, new intelligence-security agencies have been created, which today total 16. According to a report, the central of the country's intelligence community remains the Ministry of Intelligence while the Revolutionary Guards Intelligence Unit, the Military Intelligence Unit, the Police Intelligence Unit and the Intelligence Security Unit of the Revolutionary Guards are the key intelligence services in the country.

The modern history of Iran's intelligence services begins in 1953, after a coup d'état followed by the gradual accession of Pahlavi. His force was based on the efficiency of the National Intelligence and Security Organization - SAVAK (the abbreviation of Sazeman-e Ettela'at va Amniyat-e Keshvar), whose director was under the authority of the prime minister. With Ayatollah Khomeini, more than 700 followers have been initiated in Lebanon and served at the creation of the Islamic Revolutionary Guards Corps (IRGC) on 5 May 1979. After 1981, SAVAK was dissolved (61 high rank intelligence officers were killed) but its successor, SAVAMA (Sazman-e Ettela'at va Amniat-e Melli-e Iran) took over its responsibilities. It was reorganized by the Military Revolutionary Court in 1984 and became the current intelligence ministry - MOIS.

The Ministry of Intelligence and Security

The Ministry of Intelligence and Security (MOIS), known as VEVAK (Vezarat-e Ettela'at va Amniat-e Keshvar), is the first domestic civilian intelligence service of the country with approximately 15,000 employees (in 2006). MOIS is a ministry of the government and the director of this service is a minister in the government of the country, under the authority of the President. Thus, the Iranian President, elected by people's vote and approved by the clerics, has considerable powers over the intelligence activities of MOIS. The minister of intelligence is a member of the Supreme National Security Council and is always a cleric, which means that the Supreme Leader has a great influence in his appointment and closely watches his performances.

MOIS officers are recruited only from the Shiites, true believers of the doctrine "velayat-e-faqih". According to sources, their loyalty is often tested during their training in the centers form the north of Teheran and Qom. Before training, all the recruits are thoroughly "cleared out", which, in most of the cases refers to the careful check-up of their past, performed by counterintelligence officers. After training, intelligence officers are sent to undercover posts, as it happens with all the intelligence services in the world.

Iran has important intelligence departments in all its foreign missions and embassies. Foreign agents can hold official positions within MOIS and IRGC and they are recruited mostly from other Muslim communities. To this purpose, there are special departments of MOIS that recruit agents from the Persian Gulf, Yemen, Sudan, Lebanon, Iraq, the Palestinian territories, Europe, South and East Asia, North and South America.

The domestic responsibilities of MOIS are more important than the foreign ones. For example, MOIS officers supervise the ethnical minorities from Iran and infiltrate within secret demonstrations and protests. They have in view mostly Balochi, Kurds, Azeri and Arabs and they try to identify the dissidents. Another domestic MOIS mission is to monitor drug trafficking though the organization is less involved in narcotics than the IRGC.

The foreign operations of MOIS in the gathering of intelligence are done according to the methodology of SAVAK, learned from the CIA and Mossad. MOIS also performs misinformation campaigns, learned from the KGB after the Islamic revolution. The priorities of MOIS in foreign operations are: to monitor, infiltrate and control dissident Iranian groups; to initiate connections and networks for an increased influence; to carry out terrorist and military operations; to identify any type of foreign threat, especially the ones connected to Iran's nuclear program and presently focusing on Israel and USA; to disseminate false intelligence (misinformation) in order to protect Iran and its future interests; to acquire new technologies for defense as well as spare parts for the existing equipment.

Iran's misinformation operations have a wide range of manifestations. They are called "nefaq" - which means discord in Arabic, and are used in order to discredit reformist and opposition groups from other countries as well as to draw attention and create confusion within foreign powers about the Iranian military and intelligence capacities.

The foreign responsibilities of MOIS also included the assassination of dissidents abroad but, presently, this responsibility has reduced. New responsibilities occurred, referring to subversive activities and the export of revolutions abroad. Iran currently extends its connections with groups from Algeria and with the Taliban group from Afghanistan. Despite the ideological differences, they use similar tactics and have common global goals as far as the fight against the non-Islamist influence is concerned.

The Islamic Revolutionary Guard Corps

The Islamic Revolutonary Guard Corps (IRGC) is called in Arabic "Sepah-e Pasdaran-e Enghelab-e Islami", namely "The Islamic Revolutionary Guard Corps". It is Iran's second intelligence service. It is as powerful as MOIS and possibly even more powerful than the other service. IRGC was founded in 1979 by a decree issued by Ayatollah Khomeini as a guard of the new regime. According to Article 150 from the Constitution of Iran, IRGC operates as a "guarantor of the Revolution and of its achievements". For that purpose, the Supreme Leader placed under political control all the levels of the organization.

This Iranian intelligence and security service comprises three elements: the Quds Force, the Intelligence Office and the Basij Force. From the point of view of its organization, IRGC is more like a military force than a security and intelligence service since it includes air forces, navy forces and ground forces. At the same time, IRGC is a social, political and business organization, which, can be identified in the entire Iranian society, produces a large number of political and business leaders and is involved in various domains from the Iranian economy.

The intelligence departments of IRGC appear to be more active at a domestic level while at an international level, the Quds Force is the key operational group. After KGB, this group could be the most efficient group in subversive operations. The IRGC holds a singular position - an elite military organization with major intelligence capabilities - and therefore it is regarded as the military backbone of the state. Before 1984, when MOIS was completed, the IRGC was the most active Iranian intelligence organization both within the country and abroad. After the creation of MOIS, IRGC remained in the "shadow" of the intelligence organization, with a security division that operates mostly as a unit of domestic intelligence by monitoring and arresting dissidents and separatists and sending them to prisons controlled by IRGC.

The Quds Force is one of the elements of IRGC that performs undercover foreign operations. It is known as the organization "beyond frontiers" (Birun Marzi) or "The Department 9000". The force was created by Article 154 from the Constitution of Iran. The word "al-Quds" is the Arab name of Jerusalem and the name given to the force refers to the fact that one day it will liberate the holy city. The operations of the force are led by the General Staff of the Quds Force for the Export of the Revolution, a group that includes numerous directorates responsible for operations in Iraq, the Palestinian territories, Lebanon, Jordan, Turkey, India, Afghanistan, North Africa, the Arabic Peninsula, the former Soviet nations, western countries including the United States of America, France, Germany and Holland.

The Quds Force also performs counseling operations in Bosnia, Chechnya, Somalia and Ethiopia. One of the most important missions of IRGC - the Quds Force is to train Hezbollah's special operations department, which is the elite force of the movement. In the recent years, the Ouds Force deployed important operations in Iraq and Afghanistan.

The intelligence element - the Intelligence Office of IRGC - (Ettalaat-e-Pasdaran) had 2,000 personnel (in 2006, but the number of personnel is on an ascending route). This element of the IRGC is responsible for the security of the Iranian nuclear program. This means that it monitors all scientists, leads the security forces from the nuclear installations, provides guard against sabotages and performs counterintelligence operations in order to prevent the recruit of Iranian nuclear scientists by other countries. The other activities of the Intelligence Department of IRGC are not clear. Apparently, they also include the coordination of intelligence gathering by another element of IRGC - the Basij Force - for domestic security and for the foreign operations of the Quds Force.

The Basij Force is the instrument used by IRGC to implement domestic security measures. The Basij Force also contributes to the gathering of intelligence. Its name comes from "Niruyeh Moghavemat Basij", meaning "The Mobilization and Resistance Force" and it was founded in 1980. At the beginning of the war between Iran and Iraq, Ayatollah Khomeini issued a religious decree that stipulated that boys older than 12 can serve in the line of duty. Many of these young men were used in suicidal attacks, in human defense or as human mine detectors. Out of a total number of 3 million Basij members that fought in the war between Iran and Iraq, tens of thousands died and those who survived became IRGC agents.

It is the case of the current President Ahmadinejad, a former member of Basij and former agent of IRGC. If IRGC is considered to be an elite military force with highly-trained personnel, the Basij Force is more like a paramilitary force of amateurs whose members are almost entirely untrained civilian volunteers, grouped into a large number of units, ranging from surveillance units to a certain type of National Guard. According to a special report, Hussein Hamadani, the commander of Basij, proudly sustains that the militia has immense intelligence sources, the so-called "36-million intelligence network".

The structure of Basij is slightly similar with the structure of a communist party from certain totalitarian states. There are several levels of society: every Iranian city of a considerable size is divided into two "areas" or "regions" whereas in the small Iranian towns and villages there are "cells" organized as social, religious and governmental bodies. There are also Basij units for students, workers and members of the tribes. Basij also created "Ashura Brigades" for men and "al-Zahra Brigades" for women. As far as their involvement is concerned, the members of Basij are considered to be "permanent", "active" and "special". Their recruitment is done by local mosques by informal selection committees of the local leaders. The leaders of the mosques are considered to be the most influential members of the committees.

Basij had 90,000 active members and 300,000 reserves in 2005 with the possibility to augment these troops to 1 million people or more. Due to its success, the force clearly established its role and, de facto, is considered to be the domestic police force of the regime. Iran's official police (Law Enforcement Forces - LEF) could not handle the protests from Ashura in December 2009 and Ayatollah Khomeini was forced to assign missions to Basij Force, being more appropriate to the situation due to the devotion of its members. Nevertheless, the Basij Force is highly adaptable to all existing conditions and to all possible dangers. They are also very familiar to operation areas because the members of the force originated from many of these areas.

Consequently, the Basij Force acts promptly and proves increased flexibility in all its missions. STRATFOR analysts consider that since IRGC is said to have a wide range of Basij informers, it turned into "the 911 security force of Iran, capable of gathering intelligence and responding to any incident, at any moment in order to provide safety to the regime"

Military Intelligence

Similar to all the conventional military forces, Iran's conventional armed forces (Artesh) have their own joint military intelligence capability. The structure under discussion is J2 and it is responsible for traditional tactical intelligence, having personnel and officers from all the services of the armed forces, including IRGC and certain law enforcement entities. J2 is also responsible for all the operations of planning, intelligence and counterintelligence, the security of the armed forces and the coordination of intelligence in all the regular services, fighting units of IRGC and police units that have been assigned with military responsibilities.

The Ministry of Interior

The Ministry of Interior and the Law Enforcement Forces (LEF) also represent other components of Iran's intelligence and security services. The Ministry of the Interior subordinates Iran's police forces, officially founded in 1991, when the urban police of the country, the rural gendarmerie and the revolutionary committees have merged. According to the Iranian law, the Law Enforcement Forces have personnel of 40,000 people and they are officially responsible for domestic and frontier security. In time, these services focused on basic police operations and serve as the first line of defense while the Basij Force is primarily responsible for the suppression of civilian revolts.

Intelligence Coordinating Council

The Council for Intelligence Coordnation was set up in 1983 and is run by the Minister of Intelligence. It brings in numerous influential people in Iran, among them Iran's prosecutor-general and the heads of various intelligence agencies. Over the past year, the CIC has met regularly, compiling dossiers on issues ranging from "threats in cyber space," security conditions in various regions and other potential intelligence threats Iran might face.

Power Struggle

But the strength of the intelligence wing of the Guards is not popular with everyone: the power struggle between it and the Intelligence Ministry has a long turbulent history, as does friction and fierce competition between intelligence units functioning under these larger umbrella groups. Politicians and experts have been quick to point out how this rivalry — often vicious and always complex — compromises the country's intelligence initiatives. Most recently, Ali Younesi, an advisor to President Hassan Rouhani, complained there is no coordination between the various agencies.

In 2000, reformist candidates, who held the majority in parliament, introduced a bill to increase the powers of the intelligence ministry as Mahmoud Ahmadinejad began his presidency. Shortly after, Ahmadinejad made plans to reduce the number of operating intelligence agencies, though the goal was never realized.

During his presidency, Mahmoud Ahmadinejad removed an official at the Intelligence Ministry, Mohseni-Ejei, and later took steps to remove the intelligence minister, Heidar Moslehi, against the wishes of the Supreme Leader, who immediately re-instated him. Although Moslehi demanded an end to competition between intelligence agencies in 2012, a website close to Ahmadinejad accused him of double-dealing in 2011.

"Moslehi's management experience comes mostly from working for the Revolutionary Guards," the site reported. "He has had meetings with the members of a security-economic gang and he wants to implement their wishes at the intelligence ministry." When Esfandiar Rahim Mashaei, Ahmadinejad's Chief of Staff, took steps to set up a parallel intelligence organization, he came under attack by hardliners. At the time, they called for a centralized intelligence organization to replace the intelligence ministry.

"Whenever others have tried to perform the main duties of the intelligence ministry, the results have been disastrous," said Ali Younesi, Rouhani's Intelligence Minister, in February 2014. Influential Tehran MP Ali Motahari has also been quick to point out the dangers of the Revolutionary Corps meddling in intelligence matters. "Sometimes the Revolutionary Corps steps outside the border of its duties," he told a gathering of political activists in June. "For example, they must not interfere in matters of intelligence."

It is not the first time he has spoken publicly about interference, and, in the case of the 2009 presidential election, he drew a distinct line between Revolutonary Guards intelligence and violence. On August 11, 2009, he wrote to Hossein Shariatmadari, the managing editor of the hardliner daily Kayhan, criticizing the actions of the Guards. "When we give the management of the recent crisis to people like Taeb [the head of the Revolutionary Corps Intelligence Unit at the time], who is more intimate with a nightstick than thinking and reason, the result would be like this."

Over the years, a range of politicians have pointed to dysfunctional relationships and the potential dangers of a splintered intelligence network. In September, former intelligence minister, Mohammad Reyshahri (who held office from 1984-1989) told Fars News Agency that during his time there, the ministry operated with no less than seven separate units, or "seven stripes" as he called them. "During my last days in the intelligence ministry I came to the conclusion that it should be placed under the supervision of the regime's highest authorities," he said. "the Imam accepted this but issues arose which I don't want to talk about and that prevented it."

In his 2010 memoir, "Defense and Politics", former president Hashemi Rafsanjani recalled the difficulties intelligence officials repeatedly faced during his time in office, with the Reyshahri complaining in 1987 that the disparate intelligence units made it difficult to centralize intelligence activities. According to Rafsanjani, Reyshahri had cited internal problems within the Revolutionary Guards and clashes between the Guards and the ministry, recommending that the latter be restructured and run the judiciary. Rafsanjani recalled power struggles between the two groups, with the Revolutionary Guards pushing for more power and ministry officials calling for greater restrictions on the extent of the Guards' reach. Intelligence Ministry officials argued that operations should be consolidated, and that the ministry should oversee it.

The struggle — and attempts to achieve a balance between the ministry and the Revolutionary Guards — continued in this fashion until 1988, Rafsanjani recalls in his memoir. Shortly afterwards, Reyshahri reiterated his belief that the constitution be amended so that the ministry would be under the Supreme Leader's supervision, and ultimately become an organization that could carry out its work without the approval of parliament.

With the introduction of the Law for Centralization of Intelligence in 1989, the ministry was given more power. Tensions between the Guards and the ministry continued during the administration of President Khatami, the height of which was the Chain Murders scandal, when "rogue" elements of the intelligence ministry murdered up to 80 dissident intellectuals between 1988 and 1998. The scandal made it possible for the destabilization of the ministry therafter, and measures were taken to decrease its power, with the creation of splinter intelligence groups and organizations, in particular the Intelligence Unit of the Revolutionary Corps.

Some officials deny that such a power struggle exists, accusing sections of the media of fomenting fear and trying to paint a picture of an unbalanced, ineffective intelligence apparatus. "We don't work in conjunction with any other organization," Revolutionary Guards Spokesman Commander Sharif said in July 2012. "It's the hostile media that is trying to convince the public that we have an organization that is equally as powerful as the Intelligence Ministry. This is just the enemy making false accusations."

But Ali Saeedi, the Supreme Leader's representative at the Revolutionary Guards, acknowledged its role in intelligence matters in August 2009. "Intelligence activities are a necessary part of the Revolutionary Corps work. It is coordinated with other parties and higher authorities and it is in no way harmful."

Whatever their differences, one thing cannot be denied: Ayatollah Khamenei holds the power, whatever the name of the unit or the umbrella organization. "The intelligence ministry and myself worked under the supervision of the Supreme Leader," former Intelligence Minister Mohammadi Reyshahri told Fars News Agency. "During those years if anybody wanted to consult me I would tell them that the Supreme Leader needed to approve."

Ayatollah Khamenei chooses the majority of the units' senior directors and staff, and he can oversee any aspect of operations he deems appropriate. It is safe to assume that he sees no need to centralize operations, and that keeping a strong hold over disparate agencies affords him the most sustainable — and easy to manage — power. As individual intelligence agencies gain even more power, these gains transfer directly to the Supreme Leader, leaving elected leaders, like President Rouhani, with fewer avenues to negotiate their own influence.

VEVAK

The Iranian intelligence service is called the Ministry of Intelligence and Security (MOIS), or Vezarat-e Ettela'at va Amniat-e Keshvar (VEVAK) in Farsi. MOIS agents are known as "Unknown Soldiers of Imam Zaman, the name that Ayatollah Khomeini gave them.

The Ministry of Intelligence and Security (MOIS) uses all means at its disposal to protect the Islamic Revolution of Iran, utilizing such methods as infiltrating internal opposition groups, monitoring domestic threats and expatriate dissent, arresting alleged spies and dissidents, exposing conspiracies deemed threatening, and maintaining liaison with other foreign intelligence agencies as well as with organizations that protect the Islamic Republic's interests around the world.

MOIS is the most powerful and well-supported ministry among all Iranian ministries in terms of logistics, finances, and political support. It is a non-military governmental organization that operates both inside and outside of Iran. Intelligence experts rank MOIS as one of the largest and most dynamic intelligence agencies in the Middle East.

Although Islamist hard-liners in Iran are in charge of the ministry under the guidance of Supreme Leader Ayatollah Ali Khamenei, the organization encompasses a mixture of political ideologies. Every minister of intelligence must hold a degree in ijtihad (the ability to interpret Islamic sources such as the Quran and the words of the Prophet and imams) from a religious school, abstain from membership in any political party or group, have a reputation for personal integrity, and possess a strong political and management background.

According to Iran's constitution, all organizations must share information with the Ministry of Intelligence and Security. The ministry oversees all covert operations. It usually executes internal operations itself, but the Quds Force of the Islamic Revolutionary Guards Corps for the most part handles extraterritorial operations such as sabotage, assassinations, and espionage. Although the Quds Force operates independently, it shares the information it collects with MOIS.

The ministry has a Department of Disinformation, which is in charge of creating and waging psychological warfare against the enemies of the Islamic Republic.

Iran's ability to collect covert information is limited; specifically, its signals intelligence capability represents only a limited threat because it is still under development. Even though Iran has created a well-equipped counter-intelligence system to protect its nuclear program, it appears that other countries' operatives still succeed in infiltrating the system, as well as some other parts of Iran's intelligence apparatus.

MOIS's internal activities are a priority unless it is deemed necessary for MOIS to become involved directly in external operations. It is possible that the Supreme National Security Council or the Supreme Leader determines MOIS's external operations. MOIS has a proven record of accomplishment in the execution of these functions. In carrying out its constitutional duties, MOIS conducts liaison with other foreign intelligence agencies as well as with organizations such as Lebanese Hezbollah that protect and promote the Islamic Republic's foreign agenda.

As an official Iranian government agency, MOIS is overwhelmingly staffed by Iranians. Until the reelection of President Mahmoud Ahmadinejad in 2009, most MOIS personnel were not uniformly hard-line Islamists, although they were vetted for ideological conformity. For example, in an article on the Fars News Web site in July 2005, the former minister of intelligence and security, Ghorbanali Dorri Najafabadi, said that when he consulted the former foreign minister, Ali Akbar Velayati, about whether to accept an offer from President Mohammad Khatami (president, 1997–2005) to become head of MOIS, Velayati told him "the Ministry of Intelligence is like a city which is governed by various insights and trends."

MOIS operates under the direct supervision of Iran's Supreme Leader, Ayatollah Khamenei, who claims to be the leader of the Muslim world. As noted above, MOIS agents are known as "Unknown Soldiers of Imam Zaman," who is the Twelfth Imam in the succession of Islamic leaders of Shi'a Muslims. However, the organization is not bound by Shi'a beliefs. To advance its goals, MOIS recruits individuals regardless of their beliefs, including Arabs or Jews to spy in Israel. For example, the deputy minister of MOIS, Saeed Emami, was appointed to a key position in the ministry because of his family record, despite allegedly being Jewish by birth.

Back in 1979

After the 1979 Islamic Revolution, Iranian intelligence functioned like intelligence organizations in every other revolutionary country—it identified and eradicated opponents and defectors inside and outside of the country. Thus, collecting information was not the priority. At this time, the PLO was providing the most foreign information to the Iranian government.

However, the Soviet KGB allegedly used this exchange of information to feed the revolutionary government inaccurate information as a way of complicating the United States–Iran relationship more than was already the case after the Revolution.

From the beginning of the Revolution in 1979, internal security was in the hands of Islamic Revolutionary Kumitehs (literally, committees), which Ayatollah Khomeini ordered to be formed because of concerns that a police force might be more loyal to the shah than to the new revolutionary regime. People established Kumitehs in their neighborhoods in places such as police stations, mosques, and youth centers. In addition to having responsibility for security, each Kumiteh had a unit to gather information (intelligence) on its neighbors.

Ayatollah Mohammad Reza Mahdavi Kani, who was one of the revolutionaries close to Ayatollah Khomeini, was in charge of the Kumitehs. Kumitehs may have operated under the Ministry of Interior. Other groups were involved in gathering information as well, including judges who were in charge of cases dealing with sabotage by opposition groups and with counter-intelligence.

The interim government and the Revolutionary Council formed by Ayatollah Khomeini to lead the Revolution while he was exiled in Paris endeavored to revive parts of SAVAK, especially its eighth directorate, a counterintelligence unit in charge of monitoring foreign embassies and detecting espionage. This directorate focused on Eastern Bloc countries, in particular the Soviet Union, and Arab states.

After the Revolution, Dr. Ebrahim Yazdi, the first minister of the revolution, broadened the directorate's jurisdiction by focusing on more countries and by continuing to use SAVAK personnel. In 1979–80 the revolutionary government created a variety of small agencies, but the most distinctive and prestigious was the National Intelligence and Security Agency (Sazman Ettela'at va Amniat Melli Iran—SAVAMA).

It was built on SAVAK's foundation. SAVAMA successfully used the same methods as SAVAK to collect foreign intelligence, while the Islamic Revolutionary Guards Corps (IRGC) was established to guard the Revolution and deal with domestic threats. Later, the IRGC became involved in foreign intelligence operations.

The Iranian intelligence apparatus operated relatively successfully at the beginning of the revolutionary era. In July 1980, it uncovered the Nojeh Coup, an attempt to overthrow the new government by air force officers loyal to the shah. Then, the number of security and intelligence agencies increased dramatically, causing disorder in the intelligence system.

As a consequence, Mohammad Ali Rajaei, the second president of the Islamic Republic of Iran, formed the Prime Minister's Intelligence Office (Daftar-e-Ettela'at Nokhostvaziri) in 1981. At this time, intelligence responsibilities were divided among the Prime Minister's Intelligence Office, the IRGC, the army, the Kumitehs, and the police force.

In August 1983, parliament approved the formation of the Islamic Republic of Iran's Ministry of Intelligence and Security by merging three organizations that had had four continuous years of experience in dealing with foreign intelligence services and confronting antirevolutionary groups. The three intelligence organizations, which had been operating separately since 1979, were IRGC intelligence, the Kumitehs, and the Prime Minister's Intelligence Office. At that time, many former SAVAK agents were granted amnesty by religious leaders so that MOIS could benefit from their experience. Specifically, SAVAK agents were needed to boost Iran's intelligence capacity to deal with the war with Iraq in the 1980s.

The new ministry was charged with the development of a strong intelligence capability that could confront the intelligence agencies of Iran's enemies. These foreign agencies had penetrated antirevolutionary groups, and some had also infiltrated vital parts of the government during the Iran–Iraq war. Furthermore, the government had to deal with dissidents outside of the country who constantly opposed the Iranian government.

Targeting externally based Iranian opponents of the Revolution was one of the main objectives of MOIS in the 1990s. The ministry was responsible for many terrorist attacks and assassinations of dissidents during this decade, such as the assassination of Shahpour Bakhtiar (the last prime minister under the shah).

MOIS agents also were directly involved in the collection of information for the possible assassination of Salman Rushdie, an Indian-born author who wrote The Satanic Verses. Because of the alleged un-Islamic content of the book, Ayatollah Khomeini issued a fatwa in February 1989 calling on all good Muslims to kill Rushdie and his publishers.

The assassination of four Iranian-Kurdish members of the Iranian Democratic Party of Kurdistan in Berlin at a Greek restaurant named "Mykonos" in 1992 received international attention. Kurds and other minority ethnic groups such as Baluchis, Turks, and Arabs come under MOIS's surveillance because these peoples seek independence from the central government.

The "Chain Murders" in Iran were a series of assassinations that took place in the 1990s to silence Iranian dissident intellectuals. After an investigation, MOIS took responsibility for the murders by proclaiming that some of its agents committed these crimes without its awareness. An Argentine court also blamed MOIS for enlisting Hezbollah to bomb the Israeli embassy and the Jewish center in Buenos Aires in 1992 and 1994.

However, the IRGC was responsible for these incidents, although MOIS certainly had some role in these operations. MOIS provided logistics, communication among the operatives, as well as documents needed for the operations.

For the past decade, Iran's nuclear program has brought increased scrutiny by Western intelligence operatives in Iran. In return, MOIS has become more focused on countering foreign intelligence activities. The creation of a special counterintelligence unit and the capture of a number of alleged spies through MOIS's counterintelligence unit have in effect engaged Iran and its adversaries in an intelligence war.

According to Iran's constitution, the Supreme Leader sets the direction of foreign and domestic policies. He is commander in chief of the armed forces and controls intelligence operations. Hence, both MOIS and IRGC Intelligence, including the Quds Force, report directly to the Supreme Leader.

The president is the second-highest-ranking official in Iran. However, the constitution limits his authority in such a way that it subordinates the entire executive branch—and specifically MOIS and a small number of other ministries including the foreign and oil ministries—to the Supreme Leader.

The constitution also stipulates that MOIS is in charge of intelligence activities inside and outside of Iran. Islamic Revolutionary Guards Corps is required to comply with the policy of the Ministry of Intelligence and Security with regard to combating domestic antirevolutionary dissidents, and the IRGC is entitled to collect, analyze, and produce information to identify the antirevolutionaries by way of helping MOIS.

Thus, the IRGC and its external operational wing, the Quds Force, are required to report their activities to MOIS as the highest intelligence authority in the Islamic Republic of Iran. In return, MOIS provides logistical support and handles the communications aspect of operations involving Quds Force operatives and foreign organizations that work with the Quds Force, such as Hezbollah.

Consequently, in the intelligence field, the IRGC is highly active as well. The Quds Force (mainly in charge of extraterritorial operations beyond Iran's borders) and IRGC Intelligence are two other effective intelligence organizations of the Islamic Republic of Iran whose work parallels that of MOIS. IRGC Intelligence initially operated as a directorate called the IRGC Intelligence Directorate from the time of the establishment of the IRGC in 1980. After the 2009 presidential election, the IRGC Intelligence Directorate continued its activities in the form of an "organization" that receives orders from the Supreme Leader of Iran.

There is no clear division of powers and responsibilities between MOIS and the IRGC Intelligence Organization, and analysts believe this lack of definition of their responsibilities and their overlapping jurisdictions have caused friction between them. Apparently in some cases, the IRGC's Quds Force and IRGC Intelligence do not share information with MOIS as they are supposed to do.

There is a special section in MOIS called the Department of Disinformation that operates either as an independent directorate or under one of the following directorates.

MOIS headquarters appears to be in North Tehran. MOIS has a secret budget and is not accountable to other governmental organizations, including the cabinet or the Majles (parliament). It remains above the law, accountable only to the Supreme Leader, at present Ayatollah Khamenei.

With more than 30,000 officers and support personnel, MOIS is ranked by experts as one of the largest and most active intelligence agencies in the Middle East. The Iranian constitution prohibits MOIS agents from being members of any political group or party. MOIS agents go through an extremely stringent vetting process before they can become part of MOIS's missions and operations, which could implicate the highest government officials if exposed to the public.

There are two ways to be recruited into MOIS. One way is to take the entrance examinations in specific majors requested by MOIS at Imam Mohammad Bagher University in Tehran. This university is associated with MOIS. MOIS accepts three times more candidates than it can accommodate and then puts them through physical, intelligence, and personality tests, as well as interviews and a background investigation. The physical examination at MOIS is less rigorous than at other governmental training facilities in the army or special forces. It is a requirement to be healthy, but the intelligence and personality tests are more important than the physical test.

The Ministry of Intelligence and Security operates through a variety of methods and tactics. Agents may operate undercover as diplomats in Iranian embassies or in other occupations in companies such as Iran Air, branches of Iranian banks, or even in private businesses. It is thought that many Iranians who are employed in foreign educational organizations such as universities also may work for MOIS; because they have to go back to Iran often—perhaps for immigration issues or scholarships given by the Iranian government or for other reasons—they may cooperate with MOIS. To transfer money for operations, MOIS usually uses state-controlled banks with branches in foreign countries.

Lebanese Hezbollah and the Quds Force are also organizationally linked to MOIS. Support for Hezbollah has been one of the main objectives of Iran's foreign policy. To counter threats from Israel, Iran provides Hezbollah with logistical and material support and uses Hezbollah as a proxy in Iran's intelligence operations. Such support is usually delivered under Iranian diplomatic auspices. An assessment of Iran's intelligence services in the 1990s stated: *"The largest European Al-Qods [Quds] facility was in the Iranian embassy in Germany. The embassy's third floor had twenty Qods [Quds] employees coordinating terrorist activities in Europe... Recently, major operational centers were established in Bulgaria, and Al-Qods [Quds] has attempted to establish another operational facility in Milan."*

Most Iranian foreign officers and diplomats have worked with MOIS, the IRGC, or other security agencies. MOIS works in coordination with the Foreign Ministry in operations carried out abroad, using Iranian embassies for collecting intelligence. MOIS and Quds Force agents receive diplomatic passports through the embassies. Moreover, the Quds Force is believed to coordinate with the Ministry of Intelligence and Security through foreign embassies, charities, and cultural centers in targeted countries.

MOIS infiltrates Iranian communities outside of Iran using a variety of methods. For instance, a society called "Supporting Iranian Refugees" in Paris is used to recruit Iranian asylum seekers to spy on Iranians in France. MOIS also has agents who abduct individuals abroad, return them to Iran, and then imprison or kill them. MOIS's tactics of penetrating and sowing discord within the opposition abroad are discussed in an article on a Web site affiliated with the current Iranian government. The article ("How Do Iranian Intelligence Forces Operate Outside of the Country?") discusses how Iran uses different mechanisms to penetrate the foreign-based opposition. MOIS uses its former members and/or people willing to cooperate with the ministry.

They are sent to prison temporarily and become known as activists opposed to the Islamic Republic. After some time, no one questions their previous political activities; being a political prisoner is enough to be acknowledged as an opposition figure. Activists abroad may help get such a prisoner out of the country with the assistance of an international organization, or MOIS may send the prisoner abroad, calling him/her an "escaped dissenter." This mechanism of releasing political prisoners to go abroad sows mistrust within the opposition in exile.

The ministry also engages in disinformation. The largest department within MOIS, the Department of Disinformation, uses psychological warfare and disinformation against the government's opponents. This department is also in charge of employing psychological warfare to manipulate the media and to mislead other intelligence agencies about Iran's intelligence and military capabilities. However, it is unclear exactly where this department is located in the ministry. As a matter of course, the department may spread news, which might be 80–90 percent reliable and 10–20 percent disinformation.

These entities cooperate to block any sites that cause problems and to make sure that preferred sites continue to function. Control of the media and dealing with the opposition's internal and external media are additional MOIS responsibilities. The ministry targets television channels that advocate political and religious views antithetical to the Iranian government. MOIS also attempts to control domestic and foreign news and to pressure journalists in Iran. For instance, MOIS has requested that the government limit and control the presence of foreign journalists in Iran during future presidential elections. MOIS has warned the government not to repeat the same mistake it made in the previous controversial presidential election, which received broad coverage across the world.

National Iranian American Council

In the weeks since the Obama administration announced the perilous international Iran nuclear deal, growing attention has been paid to the network of organizations and foundations that have been actively lobbying in an effort to normalize relations between Washington and Tehran. Rightly, that network is being referred to as the "Iran lobby." The welcome and much-needed scrutiny of its workings and contacts provides a salutary lesson in how to identify enemies who present themselves as friends.

At the head of the pack is the Washington, DC-based National Iranian American Council (NIAC). Led by Trita Parsi, a Swedish-Iranian immigrant, NIAC has artfully worked itself into the center of the Iran policy debate. The organization has close relations with many liberal Democrat legislators and progressive outfits like J Street, the small Jewish-but-anti-Israel advocacy group, as well as minted foundations including the Ploughshares Fund and the Rockefeller Brothers Fund, both of which have donated generously to NIAC's coffers. Some of its alumnae, like Sahar Nowrouzzadeh, have even made it into the White House—in her case, as desk officer for Iran.

A good insight into NIAC's slipperiness was gleaned from an interview with Carl Gershman, the president of the Congressionally-financed National Endowment for Democracy. Expressing regret at his decision to fund NIAC and its Iranian partner Hamyaran, a regime-sanctioned NGO, to the tune of $200,000 between 2002 and 2006, Gershman said that NIAC had misrepresented itself: *"We weren't aware when these grants were made that NIAC were presenting themselves as a lobby...We were trying something that might be a way to help people on the inside [of Iran]. But that quickly became unworkable; the grant didn't work. Then NIAC showed itself as a lobby organization, so we have nothing to do with them anymore."*

NIAC's overarching aim is to strengthen the Iranian regime by boosting its ability to trade with America and its allies. That's accompanied by lots of airy, disingenuous talk about how economic openness leads to more accountable government, but there is precious little sign of the regime reforming itself. NIAC's agenda resonates because, as Sen. Marco Rubio correctly argued during the last GOP presidential candidate debate, the Obama administration is in retreat from the Middle East, and is thereby ceding vital strategic ground to the Iranians. Backed by the Russians, the Iranians have become adept at keeping their regional allies in positions of power and influence while, under Obama, we do the precise reverse with our own.

That NIAC has even gotten to this point speaks volumes about how the Obama administration views the world. The administration can say that its policies are about peace and multilateralism and cooperation all it wants; the net result is that the tyrants and gangsters in Moscow, Damascus, and Tehran are its primary beneficiaries.

Mossad's Covert War

Back in 2007

In an August 17 (2007) meeting, Israeli Mossad Chief Meir Dagan thanked Under Secretary Burns for America's support of Israel as evidenced by the previous day's signing of an MOU that provides Israel with USD 30 billion in security assistance from 2008-2018. Dagan reviewed Israel's five-pillar strategy concerning Iran's nuclear program, stressed that Iran is economically vulnerable, and pressed for more activity with Iran's minority groups aimed at regime change.

Assessing the region, Dagan said Israel sees itself in the middle of a rapidly changing environment, in which the fate of one Middle Eastern country is connected to another. Turning to Iran, Dagan observed that it is in a transition period. Instability in Iran is driven by inflation and tension among ethnic minorities.

Dagan said that the Gulf states and Saudi Arabia are concerned about the growing importance of Iran and its influence on them. They are taking precautions, trying to increase their own military defensive capabilities. Referring to the Gulf Security Dialogue (GSD), Dagan warned that these countries would not be able to cope with the amount of weapons systems they intend to acquire: "They do not use the weapons effectively."

Turning to the Gulf Security Dialogue (GSD), Dagan said that enhancing the capabilities of the Gulf states "is the right direction to go," especially as they are afraid of Iran. Such a U.S. commitment will be a stabilizing factor in the region. Dagan clarified that he would not oppose U.S. security assistance to America's Arab partners. He expressed concern, nevertheless, about the current policies of those partners — especially with regards to Syria and Iran. Dagan added that if those countries must choose between buying defensive systems from the U.S. or France, then he would prefer they buy systems from the U.S., as this would bring them closer to the U.S.

Five Pillar Strategy

Dagan led discussion on Iran by pointing out that the U.S. and Israel have different timetables concerning when Iran is likely to acquire a nuclear capability. He clarified that the Israel Atomic Energy Commission's (IAEC) timetable is purely technical in nature, while the Mossad considers other factors, including the regime's determination to succeed. While Dagan acknowledged that there is still time to "resolve" the Iran nuclear crisis, he stressed that Iran is making a great effort to achieve a nuclear capability: "The threat is obvious, even if we have a different timetable. If we want to postpone their acquisition of a nuclear capability, then we have to invest time and effort ourselves."

Dagan described how the Israeli strategy consists of five pillars:

A)Political Approach: Dagan praised efforts to bring Iran before the UNSC, and signaled his agreement with the pursuit of a third sanctions resolution. He acknowledged that pressure on Iran is building up, but said this approach alone will not resolve the crisis. He stressed that the timetable for political action is different than the nuclear project's timetable.
B)Covert Measures: Dagan and the Under Secretary agreed not to discuss this approach in the larger group setting.
C) Counter-proliferation: Dagan underscored the need to prevent know-how and technology from making their way to Iran, and said that more can be done in this area.
D) Sanctions: Dagan said that the biggest successes had so far been in this area. Three Iranian banks are on the verge of collapse. The financial sanctions are having a nationwide impact. Iran's regime can no longer just deal with the bankers themselves.
E) Force Regime Change: Dagan said that more should be done to foment regime change in Iran, possibly with the support of student democracy movements, and ethnic groups (e.g., Azeris, Kurds, Baluchs) opposed to the ruling regime.

Dagan clarified that the U.S., Israel and like-minded countries must push on all five pillars at the same time. Some are bearing fruit now; others would bear fruit in due time, especially if more attention were placed on them. Dagan urged more attention on regime change, asserting that more could be done to develop the identities of ethnic minorities in Iran. He said he was sure that Israel and the U.S. could "change the ruling regime in Iran, and its attitude towards backing terror regimes." He added, "We could also get them to delay their nuclear project. Iran could become a normal state."

Dagan stressed that Iran has weak spots that can be exploited. According to his information, unemployment exceeds 30 percent nationwide, with some towns and villages experiencing 50 percent unemployment, especially among 17-30 year olds. Inflation averages more than 40 percent, and people are criticizing the government for investing in and sponsoring Hamas, saying that they government should invest in Iran itself. "The economy is hurting," he said, "and this is provoking a real crisis among Iran's leaders." He added that Iran's minorities are "raising their heads, and are tempted to resort to violence."

Dagan suggested that more could be done to get the Europeans to take a tougher stand against Iran. Under Secretary Burns agreed, and suggested that Israel could help by reaching out to the Europeans. Dagan said that Israel is already doing this, and would continue to do so. Dagan reiterated the need to strike at Iran's heart by engaging with its people directly.

Voice of America (VOA) broadcasts are important, but more radio-transmissions in Farsi are needed. Coordination with the Gulf states is helpful, but the U.S. should also coordinate with Azerbaijan and countries to the north of Iran, to put pressure on Iran. Russia, he said, would be annoyed, but it would be fitting, as Russia appears bent on showing the U.S. that it cannot act globally without considering Russia.

Under Secretary Burns stressed that the USG is focused on Iran not only because of its nuclear program, but also because it supports terrorism and Shiite militias in Iraq. The U.S. approach is currently focused on the diplomatic track and increasing pressure on Iran through sanctions. Work in the UNSC helps to define the Iranian nuclear threat as one that affects international security, and not just that of Israel.

While UNSC members Russia, China and Qatar will water down efforts to increase pressure on Iran, it is still worthwhile to push for a third sanctions resolution. In the meantime, the U.S. will encourage the Europeans, Japan and South Korea to implement unilateral sanctions against Iran outside the UNSC framework. The U.S. will continue to encourage banks and financial institutions to slow down their operations in Iran and financially isolate it.

Regarding military pressure, the Under Secretary noted that the U.S. has deployed 1-2 carrier battle groups in the Gulf over the last six months, and that President Bush has stated that he will interrupt Iran's activity in Iraq. As for outreach to the Iranian people, the VOA is now broadcasting programs in Farsi, and the USG is trying to get more Iranian students to visit the U.S. to promote people-to-people relations.

Counter intelligence

In its ongoing shadow war with Israel, the Iranian side's lone "success" was the July 18 bombing of a Bulgarian bus carrying Israeli tourists — though European investigators last week officially attributed that attack to Iran's Lebanese proxy, Hizballah. That leaves the Islamic Republic itself with a failure rate hovering near 100% abroad and an operational tempo — nine overseas plots uncovered in nine months — that carries a whiff of desperation. A Tehran government long branded by U.S. officials as the globe's leading exporter of terrorism may be cornering the market on haplessness.

Within Iran's own borders, however, the story is different. Twice in the past two years Iranian intelligence has cracked espionage rings working with Israel's Mossad. In both cases, the arrests were the furthest thing from secret: announced at a news conference, each was later followed up by televised confessions broadcast on Iranian state television in prime time. Given Iran's history of trumped-up confessions, skepticism is more than justified. But the arrests appear to be solid. One intelligence official said the captured Iranians provided "support and logistics" to the Mossad operatives who carried out the assassinations of Iranian nuclear scientists.

At least four scientists were killed on Tehran's streets from 2010 to 2012, when Israel ratcheted back on covert operations inside Iran. Officially, Israel has remained silent on the killings, though government officials will coyly say they welcome the deaths. The Jewish state maintains the same ambiguous posture on other "setbacks" to Iran's nuclear program widely — and correctly, Western intelligence officials say — attributed to Mossad, from the Stuxnet computer virus, to mysterious explosions like the massive blast at a missile base, which destroyed ballistic missiles that could reach Israel.

The covert onslaught dovetails with Israel's history of reaching "over the horizon" to disarm perceived threats at a distance. To keep advanced arms from reaching Hamas and Hizballah, Israel in the past year sent warplanes to bomb convoys and arms depots in Sudan and Syria, respectively, without apparent retribution. In the case of Iran, however, experts say the audacity of Israel's covert campaign stirred Tehran to revive an espionage effort that lay largely fallow since 9/11. The Spy vs. Spy contest that ensued would prove woefully one-sided, even in the third-world countries where Iran chose to strike, hoping to avoid heightened security awareness in the developed world. In the end, its only success came inside Iran, where the secret police operate without inhibition.

Killings

The shadow war may have started on Jan. 15, 2007, the day Ardeshir Hosseinpour passed away. Hosseinpour was a specialist in electromagnetics at the Nuclear Technology Center in the city of Isfahan, Iran, but his death might have escaped notice had Iran's government not kept it under wraps for almost a week, finally attributing it to fumes from a faulty heater. An online report by the American private intelligence firm Stratfor suggested another cause — radioactive poisoning — and hinted that Mossad's Caesarea section was back in business.

Caesarea, named for an Israeli beach town that dates back to Roman times, is the operations branch of Israel's secret service, most notoriously responsible for the assassinations of some two dozen Palestinians (and an innocent waiter) after the 1972 Munich Olympics. Assassinations are carried out by a very small unit dubbed Kidon, the Hebrew word for "tip of the spear." Kidon operates at a remove from the legions of Mossad employees working in less lethal fields.

It would have been a unit called Hatzomet, or "The Junction," that recruited Majid Fashi, a handsome young Iranian who dropped out of high school to pursue a career in kickboxing. By the account he gave on Iranian state television early in 2011, Fashi presented himself at the Israeli consulate in Istanbul in 2007 and was vetted for a solid year before being shown any trust. Two years later, on Jan. 12, 2010, he would place a bomb on a motorbike parked on the sidewalk outside the Tehran home of Masoud Ali Mohammadi; the nuclear physicist was killed when it was detonated by remote control.

In the broadcast, Fashi accurately described the Mossad campus north of Tel Aviv. He said he had been given a laptop equipped with a second operating system and used it to communicate through online drop boxes. He was impressed by his handlers' thoroughness. At one point Fashi described studying a scale model of Ali Mohammadi's street. "It was an exact copy of the real one," Fashi said. "The tree next it, the street curb, the bridge." In a later broadcast, he was seated across from Ali Mohammadi's widow, who glared at him as he bowed his head and wept. Mossad officials were "pissed off and shocked" seeing their agent on television, the intelligence official said.

Fashi was executed in May 2012. About the same time, Iran's intelligence minister announced the arrest of 14 more Iranians, eight men and six women dubbed members of the "Terror Club" in the subsequent prime-time broadcast of that name. Filmed in shadow, and rich in atmospherics, the Aug. 5 program recreated Ali mohammadi's death and four subsequent attacks: they started with the Nov. 29, 2010 nearly simultaneous attempts on Majid Shariari and Fereydoun Abbasi, nuclear scientists driving to work when magnetic "sticky bombs" were attached to the side of their cars from passing motorcycles. Abbasi managed to escape before it detonated, saving his wife as well. Shariari was killed — a significant setback for the Iranian nuclear program where he was the top scientist, according to a Western intelligence official.

The confessed agents offered absorbing detail — they were aboard a Bajaj Pulsar, wearing helmets, when the magnet bomb stuck on the right front panel of Shariari's car exploded. The riders scrambled into the "trail car" assigned to follow the target and disappeared into the traffic of the Imam Ali Autobahn. Already gone was the car assigned to cut off and slow the car carrying the scientist. They claimed to have rehearsed on a practice track inside Israel. None of the details could be confirmed, but an intelligence official acknowledged: "Another network was taken."

The third scientist, Dariush Rezaeinejad was shot on July 23, 2011 after picking up his child at a day care; his wife described hearing shots whiz by as she chased the assailants. The most recent assassination was the Jan. 11, 2012 death of Mustafa Ahmadi-Roshan, an expert on uranium enrichment, also by a magnet bomb slapped on his car during his morning commute.

By then, Iran was trying to strike back. The task of avenging the scientists fell to the sprawling Quds Force's own covert-operations division, known as Unit 400. It took a shotgun approach, targeting Israeli diplomatic missions in a variety of countries, mostly in the developing world where the global antiterrorism mesh is not so fine. Exposed in Baku, Tbilisi, Johannesburg, Mombasa and Bangkok, the failures mounted at a pace that was itself one of the problems.

In the world of espionage, a quality covert operation can take years to pull together. Yet in the 15 months from May 2011 to July 2012, the Quds Force and Hizballah attempted 20 attacks, by the count of Matthew Levitt, a former State Department counterterrorism official. "Hizballah and the Quds Force traded speed for tradecraft and reaped what they sowed," Levitt writes in a January report for the Washington Institute for Near East Policy. "Quds Force planners were stretched thin by the rapid tempo of their new attack plan, and were forced to throw together random teams of operatives who had not trained together."

The decline in quality was so striking it initially inspired disbelief. Recall the preposterous-sounding plot weaving together a former used-car salesman, Mexico's Zetas drug gang and a bank transfer from a Revolutionary Guard account to assassinate Saudi Arabia's ambassador — by bombing a Washington restaurant? A year on it looks like the new normal.

In Bangkok, an Iranian agent entered a courtroom in a wheelchair, having accidentally blown his legs off while fleeing police. A January alert issued by Turkish intelligence was light on specifics but quite certain the Quds operatives would be staying in five-star hotels.

"There's a number of reasons that Iranian intelligence has suffered," says Meir Javedanfar, an Iranian-born analyst who lectures at the Interdisciplinary Center in Herzliya, Israel. "No. 1," he says, "is the 2009 uprisings in Iran." The street protests over a fraudulent election undermined the perceived legitimacy of the state among people who once would work for it, including in its secret services. "People less and less see it as a nationalist endeavor and more as a Khamenei-related project to strengthen himself," Javedanfar says, referring to Iran's Supreme Leader Ayatullah Ali Khamenei, who by some published accounts personally authorizes all overseas attacks.

Hard-liners further aggravated the situation by purging competent reformists from both the secret services and from Iran's embassies — crucial to a force expected to work undetected abroad. "Basically the Quds Force doesn't cooperate with the Foreign Ministry, and the Foreign Ministry isn't what it used to be either," says Javedanfar. Under President Mahmoud Ahmadinejad, 42% of ministry employees have only high school degrees. "The regime is a bigger threat to itself than Israel," he says.

Reva Bhalla, a senior analyst with Stratfor, the US private intelligence company with strong government security connections, said the strategy was to take out key people. "With co-operation from the United States, Israeli covert operations have focused both on eliminating key human assets involved in the nuclear programme and in sabotaging the Iranian nuclear supply chain," she said. "As US-Israeli relations are bound to come under strain over the Obama administration's outreach to Iran, and as the political atmosphere grows in complexity, an intensification of Israeli covert activity against Iran is likely to result."

"Israel has shown no hesitation in assassinating weapons scientists for hostile regimes in the past," said a European intelligence official, speaking on condition of anonymity. They did it with Iraq and they will do it with Iran when they can."

Mossad's covert operations cover a range of activities. Israeli and US intelligence co-operated with European companies working in Iran to obtain photographs and other confidential material about Iranian nuclear and missile sites. Israel has also used front companies to infiltrate the Iranian purchasing network that the clerical regime uses to circumvent United Nations sanctions and obtain so-called "dual use" items – metals, valves, electronics, machinery – for its nuclear programme.

The businesses initially supply Iran with legitimate material, winning Tehran's trust, and then start to deliver faulty or defective items that "poison" the country's atomic activities. "Without military strikes, there is still considerable scope for disrupting and damaging the Iranian programme and this has been done with some success," said Yossi Melman, a prominent Israeli journalist who covers security and intelligence issues for the Haaretz newspaper.

Mossad and Western intelligence operations have also infiltrated the Iranian nuclear programme and "bought" information from prominent atomic scientists. Israel has later selectively leaked some details to its allies, the media and United Nations atomic agency inspectors.

But Vince Canastraro, the former CIA counter-terrorism chief, expressed doubts about the efficacy of secret Israeli operations against Iran. "You cannot carry out foreign policy objectives via covert operations," he said. "You can't get rid of a couple of people and hope to affect Iran's nuclear capability."

The day after

A Time Magazine report revealed that Israeli intelligence services have scaled back their covert operations inside Iran. According to senior security officials who spoke to the magazine, operations have been reduced in areas such as high-profile missions, including assassinations and detonations at Iranian missile bases, as well as in recruiting spies inside the Iranian nuclear program, and efforts to gather on-the-ground intelligence.

The report further states that according to one official, the reductions have caused "increasing dissatisfaction" inside the Mossad, Israel's intelligence agency. Another official credits the reduced activities to the reluctance of Prime Minister Benjamin Netanyahu, who the official says is worried about the outcome of the operations being discovered.

Scaling back covert operations against Iran carries costs especially as Iran hurries to disperse its centrifuges into facilities deep underground. In one intelligence finding, an Israeli official says Iran itself estimates that sabotage to date has set back its centrifuge program by two full years. The computer virus known as Stuxnet is only the best known of a series of efforts to slow the Iranian program.

That effort involves a variety of governments besides Israel, involving equipment made to purposely malfunction after being tampered with before it physically entered Iran, says the report. The setbacks have prompted Iran to announce it would manufacture all components of its nuclear program itself – something outside experts are highly skeptical Tehran has the ability to actually do.

Mujahideen-e-Khalq (M.E.K.)

The roots of the MKO lie in the early 1960s. For years, clerical and feudal interests had blocked real reform in Iran. In 1961, under pressure from the Kennedy administration, the Shah appointed as prime minister 'Ali Amini, an Iranian aristocrat and former ambassador to the United States, whom Washington respected as a reformer. Amini began to challenge the traditional classes and interest groups who had long hampered reform. In January 1962, the Shah decreed Iran's first real land reform.

The Shah assumed the mantle of reforming crusader. He launched "the Shah-People Revolution," better known as the "White Revolution." Its six points were: land reform, nationalization of forests, sale of government-owned factories to finance land reform, women's suffrage, a Literacy Corps in which conscripts could serve as an alternative to the army, and distribution to workers of part of factories' profits. Such reform cut deep into the fabric of Iranian society, angering social conservatives, clerics, and xenophobic nationalists.

Against this backdrop and angered by both the growing secularization of Iranian politics and the influx of foreigners, engineer and Islamic activist Mehdi Bazargan formed the Liberation Movement of Iran. His goal was to combine Iranian nationalism with Islamism. "*We refuse to divorce religion from politics… because Shi'i Islam is an integral part of our popular culture*," the group stated in its inaugural declaration. Ayatollah Mahmud Taleqani, a free-thinking and modernizing cleric introduced to Marxist thought while imprisoned in the 1930s, became a mentor to Bazargan who, in turn, would become provisional prime minister during the first days of the 1979 revolution.

In July 1962, Amini resigned in anger over both the Shah's military spending and anger at what he considered the stinginess of other U.S. aid. Chaos reigned supreme. The ayatollahs seized the initiative. Islamic groups marched against social reforms and the new laws which restricted the clergy's traditional privileges. Ayatollah Ruhollah Khomeini rose to prominence as the head of the clerical opposition.

By 1963, what little tolerance the Shah had for the opposition evaporated. On June 5, 1963, he ordered Khomeini's arrest. Rioting erupted and ended only after the police killed several hundred students and demonstrators.

Ironically, even as the Shah's crackdown sent oppositionists underground, his reforms catalyzed their growth. State scholarships enabled a far greater range of Iranians to receive higher education than at any previous time in history. University campuses became incubators of opposition. Young radicals looked abroad and drew inspiration from revolutionary movements in Algeria, Vietnam, Cuba, and elsewhere.

Following the 1963 crackdown, Bazargan's Liberation Movement splintered. While older members drew inspiration from the left-leaning nationalist and ousted Prime Minister Muhammad Musaddiq who flirted with mob violence but did not sanction terrorism, many younger members argued political reform impossible and embraced armed struggle. These younger members, including a University of Tehran political science student named Masud Rajavi, coalesced into a discussion group which, in 1965, would form the Mujahedin al-Khalq. It would be another seven years before the MKO would emerge from its self-imposed veil of secrecy and declare itself to the wider world.

The MKO preached a combination of Marxism and Islamism. They argued that not only did God create the world, but he also set forth a historical evolution in which a classless society would supplant capitalist inequity. Such a radical re-interpretation of Islam bred division, not only with the secular and capitalist state, but also with the traditional, conservative clergy which resented the MKO argument that "Shi'i 'ulama [religious scholars], just like the Sunnis, have failed to grasp the real essence of Qur'anic dynamism." Rajavi and other MKO ideologues reinterpreted religion to justify terrorism. Death during armed struggle, they said, was consistent with traditional Shi'i glorification of martyrdom. They created a precedent from which they and later terrorist groups like Lebanese Hizbullah could and did justify suicide bombing, a plague which afflicts the region to the present.

In order to prepare itself for armed struggle, the MKO reached out to the Palestinian Liberation Organization. In 1970, several leading MKO, including Rajavi received terrorist training in PLO camps in Jordan and Lebanon. The group subsequently cemented links to the Libyan regime of Mu'ammar Qadhafi and to the People's Democratic Republic of Yemen, the Soviet Union's Arabian Peninsula satellite.

The MKO's first attempt to create a terrorist spectacle failed. A prison informant betrayed their plans to blow up a power station to disrupt the 1971 celebrations surrounding the 2500th anniversary of the Persian monarchy. An attempt to kidnap the Shah's nephew also failed. However, the subsequent trial and execution of those involved bolstered the prestige of the organization. At his trial, Rajavi gave a rousing anti-imperialist speech in which he accused the United States, western banks, and multinational corporations of most of Iran and the developing world's ills.

"The main goal now," Rajavi declared, "is to free Iran of U.S. imperialism." The military tribunal was harsh: They condemned 11 MKO leaders, including Rajavi, to death. The Iranian government commuted the sentences of one co-conspirator and Rajavi to life imprisonment after Rajavi's brother launched an international clemency campaign. The execution of the MKO's founders and so many early members positioned Rajavi well to consolidate organization control upon his January 1979 release.

While dealt a mighty blow, the MKO rebounded. It recruited new members in Iranian high schools, universities, prisons, and among the thousands of Iranian university students studying in Western Europe and the United States. The group also established a radio station in Baghdad from which to broadcast anti-regime propaganda into Iran. The MKO latched onto the teachings of the left-leaning Ayatollah 'Ali Shariati, who openly preached a similar but less radical message. They used Shariati's preaching as a launching point for underground discussion and indoctrination.

The imprisonment and execution of its leadership did not eviscerate the organization. It soon struck again. In May 30 and 31, 1972, shortly before President Richard Nixon's state visit to Iran, the MKO launched a wave of bomb attacks which targeted the Iran-American Society, the U.S. Information Office, the Hotel International, Pepsi Cola, General Motors, and the Marine Oil Company. They failed to assassinate General Harold Price, head of the U.S. Military Mission in Iran.

Less than three months later, they bombed the Jordanian embassy to revenge King Hussein's September 1970 crackdown on their PLO patrons. In 1973, the MKO bombed the Pan-American Airlines building, Shell Oil, and Radio City Cinema in Tehran, and assassinated Colonel Lewis Hawkins, the deputy chief of the U.S. military mission. They did not only target foreigners. In a wave of bombings that continued into 1975, the MKO group attacked clubs, stores, police facilities, minority-owned businesses, factories it accused of having "Israeli connections," and symbols of state and capitalism.

Not all was well within the MKO leadership. In 1975, the group divided into a Marxist faction that eschewed Islam, and a Muslim faction which did not. Baruch College historian Ervand Abrahamian, whose dispassionate and academic study of the MKO is the most thorough, argued that the shift of many MKO leaders to Marxism stemmed had three causes: Disillusionment with Ayatollah Khomeini, inability to win over the secular intelligentsia, and the influence of other radical groups like the Feda'iyan.

Rajavi headed the Muslim Mujahedin branch in Qasr prison. Both groups continued their attacks on government and Western targets, all the while striking at each other. While the Marxist MKO was unsuccessful in an attempt to assassinate a senior U.S. diplomat, it killed three American employees of Rockwell International.

While both MKO factions participated in the Islamic Revolution, the Muslim MKO found shelter under the banner of Taleqani and rode the Revolution to prominence. They claimed some credit for the seizure of the U.S. embassy and subsequent hostage taking, and later demonstrated against their release. The Muslim faction did not eschew Marxism. Rajavi and the MKO supported the Soviet invasion of Afghanistan, and opposed the Afghan mujahedin struggling against it.

In the wake of the Islamic Revolution, Rajavi consolidated his control over the organization. Rajavi divided the leadership into a Politburo and a Central Committee, and created a number of organizations to recruit and train new members. This proliferation of front organization, all serving an ideological and disciplined leadership, remains characteristic of the group today.

It was not long before Rajavi and the MKO came into conflict with the clerical circles surrounding Khomeini. Relations between the MKO and Khomeini had been long strained. While Khomeini's theological justification of clerical rule was a radical reworking of traditional Shi'i jurisprudence, he was otherwise conservative. He considered the MKO's blending of Islam with Marxism, as well as the group's denial of past jurisprudence, to be anathema. When an MKO delegation had visited Khomeini in Najaf in 1972, rather than offer the support they sought, he lectured them on true Islam.

Within a year of Khomeini's return to Iran, his followers began to label Rajavi and the MKO "unbelievers" and "hypocrites." The MKO, in return, accused

Khomeini of hijacking the revolution and imposing dictatorship. Prior to the Islamic Revolution, Khomeini promised the masses Islamic democracy, even as he consolidated dictatorship. The MKO sought to replicate his strategy, for practical, not idealistic, aims.

Khomeini had the upper hand, though. He closed the group's offices, banned its papers, and forced the MKO underground. The MKO was not his only target, though. As he consolidated power, he moved against President Abulhasan Bani Sadr whose independence and moderation undercut Khomeini's theocratic ambitions. While Bani Sadr did not join the MKO, he formed a tacit alliance with the group which, in turn, benefited from the President's prestige.

Both Bani Sadr and the MKO called for national protests on June 20, 1980, and demonstrators heeded their call. Perhaps a half million poured into the streets in Tehran; many more turned out in cities across Iran. But Khomeini and his supporters in the Islamic Republic Party were ready. They labeled anyone marching in support of the MKO to be enemies of God, subject to summary execution. They kept their word. Khomeini's followers killed hundreds. The warden of Evin Prison, Tehran's main political prison, bragged of his execution of teenage girls.

Khomeini's opponents responded. Terrorists—their affiliation unclear—blew up the Islamic Republic Party headquarters, killing hardline Ayatollah Mohammed Hosseini Beheshti, founder of the Islamic Republic's judiciary, and 72 party members. Khomeini used the attack as reason to accelerate his purge. A reign of terror began. Thousands perished before Islamic Republic firing squads and upon its gallows. As Khomeini consolidated control, Iranians' willingness to support for the MKO evaporated.

The MKO did not surrender, though. It drove its terrorist campaign to a fever pitch, assassinating several hundred regime officials and Revolutionary Guards, and bombing the homes and offices of clerics. The group also targeted judges who passed sentence against their members. The MKO used suicide bombers with deadly effect, killing in separate incidents the Friday prayer leaders of Tehran and Shiraz. At its peak in July 1982, the group assassinated, on average, three regime officials per day; publicly, the MKO has claimed responsibility for the murders of over 10,000 people in Iran since 1981. But while the terrorist campaign shook the Islamic Republic to its core, it also claimed many innocent victims.

Rajavi and Bani Sadr both fled to Paris during Khomeini's crackdown. While Bani Sadr and others had joined with the MKO under the banner of the National Council, such formal ties were short-lived. By 1984 the former president and many other groups left the umbrella, upset with the MKO's ideology and Rajavi's dictatorial tendencies.

Still more MKO supporters fled to Iraq, where they accepted the protection of President Saddam Hussein. What little support the group had once enjoyed in Iran evaporated, as Iranians saw the MKO rally in support of a dictator who launched a war that, by its conclusion in 1988, killed several hundred thousand Iranians. Ordinary Iranians are quite vocal in their hatred of the Islamic Republic and ridicule its current Supreme Leader 'Ali Khamene'i.

Many ask about Reza Pahlavi, the U.S.-based son of the late Shah. Others speak of other opposition groups, and many more rally to the names of the Islamic Republic's own dissidents. But, without exception, all spew venom toward the MKO. The group violence and its betrayal of Iranian nationalism lost it all popular support in Iran.

Nor did the MKO win Iraqi support. Iraqi intelligence coordinated MKO activities. Iraqi Kurds and Shi'a accuse the group of participating in reprisals against Iraqi civilians following the March 1991 uprising. According to Qubad Talabani, son of Iraqi president Jalal Talabani, "Up until the fall of the regime, they were part and parcel of the Iraqi military. And they were heavily involved in suppressing the Kurdish uprising of 1991."

While the MKO lost both its revolutionary power struggle and the battle for Iranian hearts and minds, Rajavi has worked tirelessly to reinvent the MKO's image. Again, he sought power in and sympathy from so many members' martyrdom. At first, the group reached out to its old leftist and Arab nationalist patrons in Algeria, Lebanon, and among the PLO. It also sent delegations to the Italian and Greek Communist Parties, the Indian Socialist Party, and the British Labour Party. It found a sympathetic audience among left-leaning human rights organization and academics. The group targeted European parliamentarians. More than 3,000 parliamentarians signed a 1986 petition of support.

The admission of Ayatollah Hossein 'Ali Montazeri, long-time Khomeini deputy, that Khomeini ordered the executions of 3,000 incarcerated MKO allowed the organization to further play the martyr card. The National Council of Resistance's website describes an international organization with "official contacts with most European countries... [and] amicable relations with Middle Eastern nations." The group has continued its petition drives. Congressional aides describe how the group sends pretty young women into the halls of Congress and various parliaments with innocuous petitions. Most lawmakers have little idea of the baggage the group carries. The MKO devotees get results.

The group brags, "In 1992, in a joint global initiative, 1,500 parliamentarians declared their support for the NCR as the democratic alternative to the Khomeini regime. This included a majority in the US House of Representatives." Abrahamian speculated that the MKO sought to replicate the PLO's strategy of winning recognition as the representatives of the Palestinian people through the international community. It continues to post endorsements, many taken out of context, on its website.

Within the United States, MKO members tell Congressmen, their staffs, and other policymakers what they want to hear: That the MKO is the only opposition movement capable of ousting the unpopular and repressive Islamic Republic. They are slick. Friendly lawmakers and commentators get Christmas baskets full of nuts and sweets. Well-dressed and well-spoken representatives of MKO front organizations approach American writers, politicians, and pundits who are critical of the regime.

The enemy of an adversary is not necessarily a friend, though. Such is the logic that caused State Department realists in the Reagan administration to support a dictator like Saddam Hussein. The MKO have little in their record to suggest democracy to be a goal. While they opposed the Islamic Republic only after Khomeini purged them from power, the group sought to replace Khomeini's dictatorship with its own. They omit and often deny their past anti-U.S. and anti-Western terrorism.

Today, Masud Rajavi—and his second wife Maryam—work to impose totalitarian control over its membership. Portraits of Masud and Maryam loom large in MKO demonstrations and facilities. In the West, the group forbids its members from reading anything but MKO newspapers and publications. Many MKO live in communal households and participate in mandatory study groups. In Camp Ashraf, Iraq, where many members sit in limbo following Saddam's fall, MKO minders enforce celibacy, employ cult methods to break down individual will, and shield members from unsupervised exposure to outsiders.

Prior to Iraq's liberation, there was rare interagency agreement about the MKO within the U.S. government. From Foggy Bottom to the Pentagon to the Old Executive Office Building, there was rare unanimity. As a terrorist organization closely allied with Saddam's regime, the MKO should be considered combatants if they raised arms, and prisoners if they did not. The Islamic Republic might want the group for crimes both real and imagined, but the fate of MKO stranded in Iraq would ultimately rest with the new Iraqi judiciary, which might want to try individual members for atrocities committed in 1991.

During Iraq's liberation, U.S. troops surrounded Camp Ashraf, the main MKO base in Iraq. Those MKO who did not flee during the war stood down. The U.S. military confined 3,800 MKO "security detainees" in the Camp. The Iranian government demanded forced repatriation and, through intermediaries, offered to trade al-Qaeda members sheltering in Iran for MKO members captured in Iraq. This offer was refused for three reasons: The priority of the Iraqi judiciary in the matter, Iran's own lack of due process, and the fact that belief that Iran should turn over al-Qaeda terrorists in the interest of justice, not for a quid pro quo.

On May 10, 2003 Agence France Presse quoted General Ray Odierno, commander of the 4th Infantry Division, as saying, "I would say that any organization that has given up their equipment to the coalition clearly is cooperating with us, and I believe that should lead to a review of whether they are still a terrorist organization or not." Odierno's statement was unwise. He had no authorization to make such a comment nor did it reflect anything but his own opinion. The MKO are masters of propaganda; he was unaware of the group's history. Complacency in the face of an opponent's overwhelming firepower makes an adversary smart, not democratic.

The gaffe made, the Pentagon fumbled its response. Its policy hierarchy and public affairs machinery were more effective at editing each others' grammar than at damage control. Despite subsequent interagency clarifications, left-wing pundits and academic conspiracy theorists went into overdrive. They knowingly conflated a single general's off-hand remark into a statement of policy, and then they conflated the uniformed services with civilian staff.

"...The Neocons in the Pentagon have some sort of weird alliance with the MEK [MKO] mad bombers," University of Michigan Professor Juan Cole wrote. Cole's anti-Semitic and partisan-driven conspiracy theories played into Rajavi's hands by enabling the group to project a false image of support where none existed.

Partisan bloggers like Laura Rozen, off-kilter academics like Cole and Brown University anthropologist William O. Beeman, Knight-Ridder and Washington Post correspondents, and New York Times' columnists, repeated the story, substituting hypothesis for fact, citing each other and justifying their beliefs with anonymous sources. None can produce an iota of evidence. While the MKO has the support of a handful of congressmen and a small number pundits, Rajavi has no support in the power centers of Washington. Nevertheless, he bolsters his supporters' morale and basks in the claim of support, however false.

Even in the era of resurgent realism, some issues should remain absolute. Terrorism, the deliberate targeting of civilians for political gain, should never be acceptable. Mitigating factors do not exist. True, in August 2003 the MKO exposed Iran's covert nuclear enrichment program. It continues to penetrate Iran's defenses and assassinate its opponents. This, though, is more a result of corruption and the Islamic Republic's crumbling control over its periphery. The MKO—and any other group—can bribe officials and penetrate defenses.

This should not give reason, on the hundredth anniversary of Iran's Constitutional Revolution, to advance or reward Rajavi's life-long megalomaniacal quest for power and his backward blend of Marxism and Islamism. Many "monsters of the left" use the rhetoric of democracy to realize their ambition. Masud and Maryam Rajavi, and the organization over which they exert dictatorial control, are no exception. The Islamic Republic of Iran victimizes its people and threatens U.S. and regional security. The solution to the problem rests, not with empowering a group or individuals just as bad, but rather in supporting the Iranian people in their quest for liberty, freedom, and democracy.

MEK was founded in 1965 as a Marxist Islamic mass political movement aimed at agitating the monarchy of the US-backed Iranian Shah, Mohammad Reza Pahlavi. The group initially sided with revolutionary clerics led by Ayatollah Khomeini following the 1979 Islamic Revolution, but eventually turned away from the regime during a power struggle that resulted in the group waging urban guerilla warfare against Iran's Revolutionary Guards in 1981.

The organization was later given refuge by Saddam Hussein and mounted attacks on Iran from within Iraqi territory, killing an estimated 17,000 Iranian nationals in the process. MEK exists as the main component of the Paris-based National Council of Resistance of Iran (NCRI), a *"coalition of democratic Iranian* organizations, groups and personalities," calling itself a "parliament-in-exile" seeking to "establish a democratic, secular and coalition government" in Iran.

The M.E.K. had its beginnings as a Marxist-Islamist student-led group and, in the nineteen-seventies, it was linked to the assassination of six American citizens. It was initially part of the broad-based revolution that led to the 1979 overthrow of the Shah of Iran. But, within a few years, the group was waging a bloody internal war with the ruling clerics, and, in 1997, it was listed as a foreign terrorist organization by the State Department.

The Mujahedeen-e-Khalq, or the People's Mujahedin of Iran is an organization responsible for the deaths of thousands of civilians since its inception. If the US and Israel launched a war against Iran, aggressor nations would likely recognize the touted "parliament-in-exile", the National Council of Resistance of Iran, as the nation's legitimate government. The US State Department's own website which features Mujahedeen-e-Khalq as Foreign Terrorist Organization, indicates that "It is unlawful for a person in the United States or subject to the jurisdiction of the United States to knowingly provide 'material support or resources' to a designated FTO".

As the Mujahedeen-e-Khalq continually seek removal from the US list of Foreign Terrorist Organizations, the group's unpardonable offenses must not be lost to the annuls of history. While NCRI leader Maryam Rajavi would prefer to masquerade as a "pro-democracy" figure, the responsible parties of the international community must rightfully condemn the actions taken by her organization and its affiliates.

In 2002, the M.E.K. earned some international credibility by publicly revealing—accurately—that Iran had begun enriching uranium at a secret underground location. Mohamed ElBaradei, who at the time was the director general of the International Atomic Energy Agency, the United Nations' nuclear monitoring agency, he had been informed that the information was supplied by the Mossad.

The M.E.K.'s ties with Western intelligence deepened after the fall of the Iraqi regime in 2003, and JSOC began operating inside Iran in an effort to substantiate the Bush Administration's fears that Iran was building the bomb at one or more secret underground locations. Funds were covertly passed to a number of dissident organizations, for intelligence collection and, ultimately, for anti-regime terrorist activities. Directly, or indirectly, the M.E.K. ended up with resources like arms and intelligence. Some American-supported covert operations continue in Iran today, according to past and present intelligence officials and military consultants.

After Saddam

Camp Ashraf

Following the toppling of Saddam Hussein, the Iraqi Army has twice attempted to enter Camp Ashraf, a "refugee camp" where the militant wing of MEK (consisting of approximately 3,200 personnel) resided under external security protection of the US military up until 2009. With the full support of the US Embassy in Iraq and the State Department, UN special representative in Iraq Martin Kobler has organized efforts to relocate MEK insurgents to a former US military base near the Baghdad airport, amusingly titled, "Camp Liberty" – to avoid violent clashes between the MEK and the Shiite-led Iraqi government.

The group has long received material assistance from Israel, who assisted the organization with broadcasting into Iran from their political base in Paris, while the MEK and NCRI have reportedly provided the United States with intelligence on Iran's nuclear program, which publicly revealed the existence of the Natanz uranium-enrichment facility in 2002.

JSOC

Although the group has been credited with the assassination of high profile US military personnel following the Islamic Revolution on multiple occasions, members of Mujahideen-e-Khalq were trained in communications, cryptography, small-unit tactics and weaponry by the Joint Special Operations Command (JSOC) at a base in Nevada starting in 2005. JSOC instructed MEK operatives on how to penetrate major Iranian communications systems, allowing the group to intercept telephone calls and text messages inside Iran for the purpose of sharing them with American intelligence.

From the air, the terrain of the Department of Energy's Nevada National Security Site, with its arid high plains and remote mountain peaks, has the look of northwest Iran. The site, some sixty-five miles northwest of Las Vegas, was once used for nuclear testing, and now includes a counterintelligence training facility and a private airport capable of handling Boeing 737 aircraft. It's a restricted area, and inhospitable—in certain sections, the curious are warned that the site's security personnel are authorized to use deadly force, if necessary, against intruders.

While senior figures in the Council on Foreign Relations describe MEK as a "cult-like organization" with "totalitarian tendencies," a cabal of elder statesmen such as former NATO Supreme Allied Commander General Wesley K. Clark, former New York City Mayor Rudy Giuliani, former 9/11 Commission Chairman Lee Hamilton endorsed the removal of the Mujahideen-e Khalq from the US State Department's list of Foreign Terrorist Organizations.

Despite the growing ties, and a much-intensified lobbying effort organized by its advocates, M.E.K. has remained on the State Department's list of foreign terrorist organizations—which meant that secrecy was essential in the Nevada training. "We did train them here, and washed them through the Energy Department because the D.O.E. owns all this land in southern Nevada," a former senior American intelligence official told me. "We were deploying them over long distances in the desert and mountains, and building their capacity in communications." A spokesman for J.S.O.C. said that "U.S. Special Operations Forces were neither aware of nor involved in the training of M.E.K. members."

The training ended sometime before President Obama took office, the former official said. In a separate interview, a retired four-star general, who has advised the Bush and Obama Administrations on national-security issues, said that he had been privately briefed in 2005 about the training of Iranians associated with the M.E.K. in Nevada by an American involved in the program.

They got "the standard training," he said, "in commo, crypto [cryptography], small-unit tactics, and weaponry—that went on for six months," the retired general said. "They were kept in little pods." He also was told, he said, that the men doing the training were from JSOC, which, by 2005, had become a major instrument in the Bush Administration's global war on terror. "The JSOC trainers were not front-line guys who had been in the field, but second- and third-tier guys—trainers and the like—and they started going off the reservation. 'If we're going to teach you tactics, let me show you some really sexy stuff...' "

It was the ad-hoc training that provoked the worried telephone calls to him, the former general said. "I told one of the guys who called me that they were all in over their heads, and all of them could end up trouble unless they got something in writing. The Iranians are very, very good at counterintelligence, and stuff like this is just too hard to contain." The site in Nevada was being utilized at the same time, he said, for advanced training of élite Iraqi combat units. (The retired general said he only knew of the one M.E.K.-affiliated group that went though the training course; the former senior intelligence official said that he was aware of training that went on through 2007.)

Allan Gerson, a Washington attorney for the M.E.K., notes that the M.E.K. has publicly and repeatedly renounced terror. Gerson said he would not comment on the alleged training in Nevada. But such training, if true, he said, would be "especially incongruent with the State Department's decision to continue to maintain the M.E.K. on the terrorist list. How can the U.S. train those on State's foreign terrorist list, when others face criminal penalties for providing a nickel to the same organization?"

Robert Baer, a retired C.I.A. agent who is fluent in Arabic and had worked under cover in Kurdistan and throughout the Middle East in his career, initially had told me in early 2004 of being recruited by a private American company—working, so he believed, on behalf of the Bush Administration—to return to Iraq. "They wanted me to help the M.E.K. collect intelligence on Iran's nuclear program," Baer recalled. "They thought I knew Farsi, which I did not. I said I'd get back to them, but never did." Baer, now living in California, recalled that it was made clear to him at the time that the operation was "a long-term thing—not just a one-shot deal."

Massoud Khodabandeh, an I.T. expert now living in England who consults for the Iraqi government, was an official with the M.E.K. before defecting in 1996. In a telephone interview, he acknowledged that he is an avowed enemy of the M.E.K., and has advocated against the group. Khodabandeh said that he had been with the group since before the fall of the Shah and, as a computer expert, was deeply involved in intelligence activities as well as providing security for the M.E.K. leadership. For the past decade, he and his English wife have run a support program for other defectors.

Khodabandeh told me that he had heard from more recent defectors about the training in Nevada. He was told that the communications training in Nevada involved more than teaching how to keep in contact during attacks—it also involved communication intercepts. The United States, he said, at one point found a way to penetrate some major Iranian communications systems. At the time, he said, the U.S. provided M.E.K. operatives with the ability to intercept telephone calls and text messages inside Iran—which M.E.K. operatives translated and shared with American signals intelligence experts. He does not know whether this activity is ongoing.

Five Iranian nuclear scientists have been assassinated since 2007. M.E.K. spokesmen have denied any involvement in the killings, but early last month NBC News quoted two senior Obama Administration officials as confirming that the attacks were carried out by M.E.K. units that were financed and trained by Mossad, the Israeli secret service. NBC further quoted the Administration officials as denying any American involvement in the M.E.K. activities. The former senior intelligence official I spoke with seconded the NBC report that the Israelis were working with the M.E.K., adding that the operations benefitted from American intelligence.

He said that the targets were not "Einsteins"; "The goal is to affect Iranian psychology and morale," he said, and to "demoralize the whole system— nuclear delivery vehicles, nuclear enrichment facilities, power plants." Attacks have also been carried out on pipelines. He added that the operations are "primarily being done by M.E.K. through liaison with the Israelis, but the United States is now providing the intelligence." An adviser to the special-operations community told me that the links between the United States and M.E.K. activities inside Iran had been long-standing. "Everything being done inside Iran now is being done with surrogates," he said.

The sources I spoke to were unable to say whether the people trained in Nevada were now involved in operations in Iran or elsewhere. But they pointed to the general benefit of American support. "The M.E.K. was a total joke," the senior Pentagon consultant said, "and now it's a real network inside Iran. How did the M.E.K. get so much more efficient?" he asked rhetorically. "Part of it is the training in Nevada. Part of it is logistical support in Kurdistan, and part of it is inside Iran. M.E.K. now has a capacity for efficient operations that it never had before."

In mid-January, a few days after an assassination by car bomb of an Iranian nuclear scientist in Tehran, Secretary of Defense Leon Panetta, at a town-hall meeting of soldiers at Fort Bliss, Texas, acknowledged that the U.S. government has "some ideas as to who might be involved, but we don't know exactly who was involved." He added, "But I can tell you one thing: the United States was not involved in that kind of effort. That's not what the United States does."

Stuxnet virus

Recent revelations connecting MEK with the Stuxnet computer virus that destroyed several hundred centrifuges in Iran's Natanz nuclear facility constitutes an act of deliberate and unparalleled sabotage. Stuxnet remains the most sophisticated malware discovered thus far, the virus targets Siemens' Simatic WinCC Step7 software, which controls industrial systems such as nuclear power plants and electrical grids from a Microsoft Windows-based PC.

The virus exploits security gaps referred to as zero-day vulnerabilities, to attack specific targets. Prior to its discovery, Stuxnet was previously undetected and remained unidentified by anti-virus software, as the malware was designed to appear as legitimate software to Microsoft Windows. Upon delivery of the Stuxnet payload, the malware manipulated the operating speed of centrifuges spinning nuclear fuel to create distortions that deliberately damaged the machines, while giving the impression of normal activities to the monitoring operator and disabling their emergency controls.

Current and former US intelligence officials, who confirm the Stuxnet virus was planted at Natanz nuclear facility by a saboteur believed to be a member of Mujahedeen-e-Khalq. By delivering the malicious payload via USB memory stick, the group was able to damage at least 1,000 centrifuges in the Natanz nuclear facility. MEK has also been accused of assassinating Iranian nuclear scientists and triggering an explosion that destroyed an underground site near the town of Khorramabad in western Iran that housed most of Tehran's Shehab-3 medium-range missiles.

Due to the intricate nature of Stuxnet coding, security experts confirm its creation must the "work of a national government agency" . Ralph Langner, an independent computer security expert who dismantled Stuxnet credited Israel and the United States with writing the malicious software designed to sabotage the Iranian nuclear program. Considering that Stuxnet targeted Programmable Logic Controllers (PLC) used in industrial plants to automate industrial operations, the malware designers required detailed knowledge of the programming language written for PLC components to successively subvert them.

It remains significant that the German electrical engineering company Siemens cooperated with one of the United States in 2008 to identify vulnerabilities in the computer controllers identified as key equipment in Iran's enrichment facilities. Intelligence experts concede that testing of the Stuxnet virus was conducted in the Dimona complex located in Israel's Negev desert, the site of Israel's rarely acknowledged nuclear arms program.

When asked about the Stuxnet worm in a press conference, current White House WMD Coordinator Gary Samore boasted, "I'm glad to hear they are having troubles with their centrifuge machines, and the U.S. and its allies are doing everything we can to make it more complicated". While former chief of the International Atomic Energy Agency (IAEA) Hans Blix challenges the IAEA's own reports on Iran's nuclear activities (accusing the agency of relying on unverified intelligence from the US and Israel), former director of US nuclear weapons production programs, Clinton Bastin, has sent an open letter to President Obama regarding the status of Iran's capacity to produce nuclear weapons .

Bastin reiterates in his letter to the President, "The ultimate product of Iran's gas centrifuge facilities would be highly enriched uranium hexafluoride, a gas that cannot be used to make a weapon. Converting the gas to metal, fabricating components and assembling them with high explosives using dangerous and difficult technology that has never been used in Iran would take many years after a diversion of three tons of low enriched uranium gas from fully safeguarded inventories. The resulting weapon, if intended for delivery by missile, would have a yield equivalent to that of a kiloton of conventional high explosives".

Alexander Gostev, chief security expert at Russia's Kaspersky Lab examined drivers used in Stuxnet and Duqu and concluded a single team most likely designed both worms, based on their interaction with the surrounding malware code. Duqu malware similarly exploits Microsoft Windows systems using a zero-day vulnerability and is partially written in an advanced and previously unknown programming language, comprised of a variety of software components capable of executing information theft capabilities highly related to Iran's nuclear program. Duqu has the capacity to steal digital certificates to help future viruses appear as secure software. Duqu's replication methods inside target networks remain unknown, however due to its modular structure, a special payload could theoretically be used in further cyber-physical attacks.

Follow the money

MEK was put on the State Department's list of Foreign Terrorist Organizations in 1997. MEK supporters suggest this was a failed political move by the Clinton administration to soften relations with Tehran. Regardless, the organization says it is now a peaceful and democratic resistance movement, one allied with the U.S in its distrust of the current Iranian regime and Iran's nuclear program. A slew of American officials, including Freeh, FBI Director at the time the terror list designation was made, and a number of military officers of the highest rank, have come to the support of MEK and lobbied for its removal from the terrorist list.

U.S. Department of Treasury opened investigations into former government officials who have been paid speaking fees by the Mojahedin-e-Khalq, or MEK, an Iranian resistance group officially listed as a terrorist organization. The subpoenaing of former Pennsylvania Governor Ed Rendell, ex-FBI Director Louis Freeh and retired Gen. Hugh Shelton has cast an harsh light on other U.S. officials, including former New York City Mayor Rudi Giuliani and former Vermont Governor Howard Dean, as well as the organization they publicly support.

A 2004 FBI investigation uncovered a glut of shady fund-raising operations. According to the report, the voracity of which has been called into question, money raised by the Los Angeles and Washington D.C. cells was transferred overseas through a complex international money laundering operation that uses accounts in Turkey, Germany, France, Belgium, Norway, Sweden, Jordan and the United Arab Emirates.

At one point, MEK was also operating charities called the Committee for Human Rights and Iran Aid, which claimed to raise money for Iranian refugees persecuted by the Islamic regime, but was later revealed to be a front for MEK's military arm, the National Liberation Army.

All of this could account for some of MEK's resources but would be unlikely to cover the exorbitant speaker fees recently doled out. Moreover, MEK supporters would claim that if true, these practices were done during a previous incarnation of the group, the middle ground between being a fully-militant organization and a refugee group under U.S. military protection in Iraq.

Almost all of the former U.S. officials who support delisting were not actually paid by MEK, but by Iranian-American cultural organizations like the Iranian American Community of North Texas and the Iranian American Cultural Association of Missouri. This network of non-profits could be the best way to track MEK's funding. According to experts, money from benefactors and pledge drives in Europe is sent to individuals in the United States, then onto front groups and finally given to American politicians. It's complicated, but according to federal law, it's still illegal.

It's much easier to move around money in Europe because MEK is no longer on the watch list, said Parsi.

None of this may matter soon. MEK has filed a federal suit that would force the State Department, which says it continually evaluates the terrorist organization list anyway, to officially review the organization's status within 30 days. Secretary of State Hillary Clinton also said that a successful transfer from Camp Ashraf to former U.S. military base Camp Liberty, which is currently underway, will help speed up any potential delisting. If that happens, former politicians like Giuliani, ex-Homeland Security Secretary Tom Ridge and former U.N. ambassador John Bolton will continue to advocate for the MEK despite criticism and possible legal ramifications.

Alana Goodman is correct to highlight the current battle between Attorney-General Eric Holder and a bipartisan array of prominent former U.S. officials who have accepted hefty honoraria from Mujahedin al-Khalq (MEK) front groups, even though the State Department lists the MEK as a terrorist group. While cultivating prominent endorsers is one front in the group's public relations battle, the largest war – and the reason the MEK has spent millions on former American officials – is for their support in its battle to be delisted as a terrorist entity.

There is no doubt that in the past, the MEK engaged in terrorism against Americans and that it has embraced a fiercely anti-Western ideology. Proponents of delisting the MEK, however, argue that the group has not engaged in terrorism against the United States or its interests for decades. The State Department may eventually be forced by the letter of the law to delist the MEK. That does not mean the group is entitled to any American support. The group's culpability in recent terrorist attacks in Iran is murkier. Still, it would be a mistake to boil the MEK issue—and the question of U.S. support—down to the terrorism listing, however. Working with the MEK is simply bad policy.

It is illegal in every sense of the word to finance them right now, said Trita Parsi, founder of the National Iranian American Council, a non-partisan community organization based in Washington. The actual sum being paid to these officials is vague, but judging by the fees handed to certain individuals, the total could be in the millions. For example, Rendell was allegedly paid $150,000 for seven or eight speeches, according to reports. Giuliani, who spoke in at a conference in Paris, France on behalf of Iranian resistance figures alongside 18 other international guests, has been known to charge up to $100,000 for a single appearance and sometimes demands private jets to charter him to appearances.

Other former U.S. officials told the New York Times that the American supporters of MEK received between $15,000 and $30,000 per speech, yet others said they made appearances for free.

Where does an organization based in an Iraqi refugee camp get so much money? While MEK has organized rallies and campaigns to have it delisted as a terrorist group in the past, it has never, by all accounts, spent the amount of money it has over the past year. Currently, there are rumors that the Israeli secret service is paying MEK to carry out assassinations of Iranian nuclear scientists.

From 1980 until the invasion of Iraq in 2003, MEK was funded by Saddam Hussein. Following the adage the enemy of my enemy is my friend, MEK joined Hussein during the Iran-Iraq War and fought viciously against the Ayatollah's forces. MEK made Camp Ashraf, which is about 55 miles north of Baghdad, its permanent headquarters in 1986.

Some estimate that Hussein was paying as much as $30 million a month for at least 10 months -- some of it allegedly run-off from the UN's failed Oil-for-Food program -- for MEK's services, which included strikes against Kurdish and Shia rebels in Iraq.

Additionally, during the Iran-Iraq War, MEK leader Masoud Rajavi -- whose wife Maryam Rajavi currently runs the National Council of Resistance of Iran, or NCRI, MEK's political arm -- allegedly took control of all of his members' assets, possessions and even their passports so they couldn't leave Camp Ashraf.